velvet rain poetry

Jaclyn Grammer

Presentation by *BookLeaf Publishing*

Web: www.bookleafpub.com

E-mail: info@bookleafpub.com

ISBN: 9789360941628

First edition 2024

For Holden,

my sweet angel

ACKNOWLEDGEMENT

Cover Photo Cred:
Tina Takes Photos

fucking king

Still trying to convince myself
Not to flee
I slowly walk the length of the crowded market
Towards the tiny cafe

I catch a glimpse of him
In the distance
Synchronously
My breath catches
My hands begin to shake

After a few additional hesitant steps
He spots me, grinning,
Opens his arms broadly
Like he is king of the fucking land

I want to vomit

lost soul

Even as the rain falls
I feel no wetness

For you cannot dampen
A soul that is already drowning

why

Tell me your side of the story
I would love to hear
I have gone mad trying to write it
The way things must appear

In your fairytale version
Where you are not the villain
Not the one to be feared
But rather the victim
The one whom we cry with
And ache for
The one we hold so dear

Tell me your side of the story
Make me understand
Walk me through the journey
Take me by the hand

I'm begging you to convince me
Please just tell me why

Why, why, why
I should give a damn

heartbreak

He walks in
With a bouquet of red roses
And a face of pride
I smile sweetly
As my heart cracks a little more

He never seems to remember

I prefer daises

the calm of night

I gaze at the moon
Wondering what life would be like
Not here

A life away
Away from you

I almost levitate
Off the ground
At the simple thought

I smile at the picture
Dancing amongst the stars

The vision of baby and me
Serene, tranquil, placid

The night air
Chills my bare arms
I hug myself
As the dream disappears
Into the darkness

without hearing a word

I hear myself talking
Fluctuating the pitch of my voice
Watching you
Dying for a sign
You might be listening

But you stopped listening years ago

You stopped paying attention
To my stories, my worries
Stopped noticing my hair
Or my new dress
You stopped as quickly as you started

You are surprised when I tell you news
News I already told you
Weeks ago
My chest pinches with frustration
My heart swells with sadness

But you have simply stopped
Stopped listening, stopped loving

Now you are talking
Louder than I ever did

Big gestures, eyes wide
Nodding you head
While watching me expectingly
Almost pleadingly
Attempting to force agreement upon me

I recognize the look
The begging behind the eyes

Without hearing a word
I stare back at you
Unresponsive

I softly smirk
Impassively
Gingerly bite my bottom lip
Turn my eyes away

I stopped listening months ago

honesty

To be honest
I am kind of intimidated by you
He stuttered

She smiled coyly
It was the best compliment
She had ever received

tea

We sit across from one another
The table small
But the distance between us immense

The cafe is crowded and eerily quiet
The absence of sound is unnerving
No music, just hushed conversations

Espresso machines vibrate loudly
Filling the void
Steam rises with hypnosis
Entrancing one to look and listen

I notice the woman, grayed hair
Braids beyond her shoulders
Peaking at us
Over top of her newspaper

I return my attention to him
Wishing he would speak softer
Listening to his complaints
About the weather

I feel her watching me

I glance her direction
Met with her stare
Unblinking, unwavering
Her eyes filled with kindness
Not judgement
I feel a calm looking into them

He is standing now
Towering over me
I tilt my head upwards
Smiling weakly
Always beneath him

He leans down
Kisses my head
I watch him exit
Disappearing in the sunshine

The door shuts
My shoulders relax
My breathing steadies

I look over at her again
Still staring
Eyes fierce and tender

I quickly glance away
Shifting my gaze down
At my undrunk tea

Now lukewarm at best

He's a lemon
I hear clearly from her direction

I look over at the woman,
Hair somehow even grayer
Than it was just minutes ago

He's a lemon
She repeats boldly
Lowering her paper

Smiling, she lifts her mug
Hands wrinkled and frail

But you already knew that,
Didn't you, love

nightmare

A scream so loud
My throat instantly burns
Fists clench
White knuckles
Glowing in the dark

Knuckles fueled with fury
Pounding against him

A frenzied howl
Enough to desquamate paint from the walls

And enough to knock him off me

My chest heaves upon extinction of the scream

As the sound vibrates
Off my eardrum
I release my hostage breath

With the first taste of blood
My tears begin to fall

The sound of his footsteps
Walking away

The echoes of him downstairs

Ice clanking in a glass

I bury my head in my pillow
Tears tasting the same as blood
Continuous warm streams of salt
Impossible to tell where one flood ends
And the next begins

A crimson satin
On my pillow and skin

And another black hole
In my heart

reflection

Are you hopeful
She asks the girl
In the mirror

The girl raises a brow
Shakes her head
Just once

Without blinking
The reflection sternly declares

Change that. Immediately.

flowers

How do flowers heal
From the storms they weather
How do they smell so sweet
And radiate in the sun
How do they continue to stand
Tall and beautiful
Like they didn't just endure
The beating of a lifetime

How do they do it

How do I become a flower

black

I'll wear black
White rose in one hand
Tissue in the other
Smile to the sweet melody
Embrace your mother
Maybe even shed a tear

I will assume the role
Feigning sadness

I'll wear black
The color of your heart
The shade of the marks
Hidden beneath my dress
A bitter remembrance of you

Fake the heartbreak
Cry how I will miss you so

I'll wear black
And finally be free

you will find her

I know your heart aches
I know your eyes cry
I know you long for her
More than anyone in the world

The search feels endless
The journey ruthless

Keep fighting
Keep loving
Keep growing
Keep wandering

You will find her

The woman you are meant to be

the love i want

If I straddle you in the kitchen
And you don't drop everything
To wrap your arms around me

I don't want it

love through tears

The sun shone bright today
Brighter than yesterday
Figuratively or literally
I am not sure
But the light reaches me
My skin, red and warm
My soul, burning from within

Walking along the street
He drops my hand
As he turns to face me
Come here
He whispers sweetly, pleadingly
He uses his fingers to wipe the tears streaming
down my face
I never knew it possible to feel such sadness and
love
In one singular moment

golden

And as I was at my most broken
You wrapped your arms around me

Like the strongest glue in the world
You bound my pieces back together

And helped me see
The golden light
Shining through
All the cracks

beautiful

She glances in the mirror, smiling
The girl in the mirror smiles back

Finally, she sees beyond her reflection

For the first time
She sees her soul

And it's beautiful

velvet rain

My arm links through his
Forcing our bodies close
I like the boots, he says, sexy

I glance down
Scuffed toes, frayed laces
I step in a shallow puddle
Water droplets form on the boots
Mud splashes on my calf

I look up at him, smiling
Our bodies separate
Only long enough to turn towards one another
He places his hand on the back of my neck
Pulling me towards him

Just as his lips touch mine
The clouds surrender
Velvet rain falls from the midnight sky

eyes of blue

It's sunny outside
It's sunny outside
The little voice squeals with glee

My body bounces slightly
As tiny feet land on the mattress
Over and over again

His body comes crashing down
As I exhaust a moan

His arm loosely around my neck
A single peck on the cheek
I love you mommy

My heart instantly warms
I stare into beautiful blue eyes
An exact reflection of my own

Tiny giggles mix with Eskimo kisses

This is the love
I have been searching for

This is the love
I never knew I needed

9 789360 941628